The INSIDE GUIDE

GLOBAL GEOGRAPHY

Exploring Sub-Saharan Africa's Geography

By Heather Smore

Cavendish Square

Published in 2026 by Cavendish Square Publishing, LLC
2544 Clinton Street Buffalo, NY 14224

Website: cavendishsq.com

Cataloging-in-Publication Data

Names: Smore, Heather.
Title: Exploring Sub-Saharan Africa's geography / Heather Smore.
Description: Buffalo, NY : Cavendish Square Publishing, 2026. | Series: The inside guide: global geography | Includes glossary and index.
Identifiers: ISBN 9781502674319 (pbk.) | ISBN 9781502674326 (library bound) | ISBN 9781502674333 (ebook)
Subjects: LCSH: Africa, Sub-Saharan–Geography–Juvenile literature. | Africa, Sub-Saharan–Juvenile literature.
Classification: LCC DT351.9 S66 2026 | DDC 916.7–dc23

Editor: Katie Kawa
Designer: Deanna Lepovich

The photographs in this book are used by permission and through the courtesy of: Cover Pav-Pro Photography/Shutterstock.com; p. 4 pingebat/Shutterstock.com; p. 6 Myroslava Bozhko/Shutterstock.com; p. 7 Marian Galovic/Shutterstock.com; p. 8 Simon Eeman/Shutterstock.com; p. 9 Teo-Inspiro International/Shutterstock.com; p. 10 Artur_Nyk/Shutterstock.com; p. 12 Raphael Mathon-Goupil/Shutterstock.com; p. 13 Fabian Plock/Shutterstock.com; p. 14 Sebastian Castelier/Shutterstock.com; p. 15 (top) Andre Silva Pinto/Shutterstock.com; p. 15 (bottom) Atlas Lion/Shutterstock.com; p. 16 Goldilock Project/Shutterstock.com; p. 18 (top) Joanna Rigby-Jones/Shutterstock.com; p. 18 (bottom) Gunter Nuyts/Shutterstock.com; p. 19 LouieLea/Shutterstock.com; p. 20 Martin Pelanek/Shutterstock.com; p. 21 Riccardo Mayer/Shutterstock.com; p. 22 Aleksandar Todorovic/Shutterstock.com; p. 24 Dirk van Rooyen/Shutterstock.com; p. 25 i_am_zews/Shutterstock.com; p. 26 Fred Marie/Shutterstock.com; p. 27 (top) KillStock/Shutterstock.com; p. 27 (bottom) Media Lens King/Shutterstock.com; p. 28 (graphic organizer) Fireofheart/Shutterstock.com; p. 28 (top left and center) Oasis World/Shutterstock.com; p. 28 (top right) Katty2016/Shutterstock.com; p. 28 (bottom left) Extezy/Shutterstock.com; p. 28 (bottom right) MyPro/Shutterstock.com; p. 29 (left) Malyshev Sergei/Shutterstock.com; p. 29 (right) mehmet ali poyraz/Shutterstock.com.

CPSIA compliance information: Batch #CSCSQ26: For further information contact Cavendish Square Publishing LLC at 1-877-980-4450.

Printed in the United States of America

CONTENTS

Shown here is a map of the continent of Africa. It is made up of many different countries and many unique, or special, geographic regions.

A CLOSER LOOK AT AFRICA

Chapter One

Like many of Earth's continents, Africa is home to many countries, **ecosystems**, and groups of people. Some people talk about Africa as if the land—and the people who live on it—are the same everywhere on the continent. This isn't true. The lands and people of Africa are incredibly diverse.

Because Africa is such a large continent, geographers often divide it into regions. The two main regions of Africa are North Africa and sub-Saharan Africa. The larger of the two is sub-Saharan Africa, which includes the lands south of the desert known as the Sahara.

A Large Landmass

Africa is the second-largest continent, and it contains about a fifth of all the land on Earth. That's about 11.7 million square miles (30.3 million sq km)—bigger than China, India, most of Europe, and the mainland United States combined!

Fast Fact

Africa is the only continent to have land in all four of Earth's hemispheres: the Northern, Southern, Eastern, and Western Hemispheres.

The Indian Ocean is located on Africa's eastern side, while the Atlantic Ocean is found off Africa's west coast. African islands are in both oceans.

The **equator** runs across the middle of Africa. This means that much of its land is in tropical, or warm, regions. However, some parts of Africa are cold enough to get snow!

The Nations of Sub-Saharan Africa

How many nations are found in sub-Saharan Africa? It depends on who you're asking. According to the **United Nations** (UN), 46 of Africa's countries are in the region. Other organizations may include more countries, so the number varies by source.

In general, to the northwest, you will find the larger countries of Mauritania, Mali, Niger, Nigeria, and Cameroon. To the northeast, you will find South Sudan, Eritrea, Ethiopia, and Kenya. In the center of the region are the Democratic Republic of the Congo, Zambia, Tanzania, and Angola. To the south, there's Zimbabwe, Botswana, Namibia,

ROOTED IN RACISM?

Some people believe that the words used to describe Africa don't always paint an **accurate** picture of the continent. For example, the term "sub-Saharan Africa" is sometimes seen as **controversial**. The countries of the region are very different from each other, but they often get grouped together under one name.

The term may have come from the racist colonial belief that sub-Saharan African countries were all the same. There's a push now to use more precise language when talking about areas and **cultures** of Africa. However, geographers often still divide continents into regions—not only in Africa, but in other parts of the world as well.

Fast Fact

Sub-Saharan Africa also includes some island nations. Islands like Madagascar and the Seychelles are off the east coast, while islands like Cabo Verde (also known as Cape Verde) are off the northwest coast.

Shown here is the view from a national park in the Democratic Republic of the Congo. This is the largest country in sub-Saharan Africa and the second-largest country on the continent. Only Algeria, which is in North Africa, is larger.

Fast Fact

The country of Djibouti is south of Eritrea, but it's often not considered part of sub-Saharan Africa. The World Bank considers it part of North Africa.

and South Africa. Many smaller countries are also found here.

Beautiful Biomes

Sub-Saharan Africa contains many different biomes. These are like neighborhoods in nature, with their own climate, plants, animals, and landforms.

The biomes of sub-Saharan Africa include valleys, mountains, rainforests, and deserts. Savannas are a very famous biome in this part of the world. These grasslands are home to lions, elephants, gazelles, and more. Many national parks and reserves have been created in this region to protect the savannas and the animals that live in this biome.

Giraffes are commonly seen on the savannas of sub-Saharan Africa.

A Growing Region

Sub-Saharan Africa is one of the most populated regions on Earth. It is home to more than 1 billion people, and the cities of this region are expanding quickly to house the growing population.

Lagos in Nigeria, located on the Atlantic coast, is home to about 21 million people in the city and its surrounding areas. It's a commercial, educational, cultural, and industrial center. Kinshasa, in the Democratic Republic of the Congo, is located on the Congo River and is home to about 17 million people. Other major sub-Saharan African cities include Dakar in Senegal, Cape Town in South Africa, and Nairobi in Kenya.

Some experts believe the population of sub-Saharan Africa could double in the next 50 years! This could cause major problems for the environment, or natural world, as crowded cities such as Lagos (*shown here*) would need to expand even more.

The desert landscape of the Sahara (*shown here*) divides the continent of Africa.

DESERTS AND WATERWAYS

Chapter Two

Sub-Saharan Africa is defined by its proximity, or closeness, to one of Africa's most famous geographic features: the Sahara. This desert forms a **barrier** between North Africa and the rest of the continent. However, Africa isn't a completely arid, or very dry, continent. In fact, sub-Saharan Africa is home to some of the longest rivers in the world.

The Largest Hot Desert

The Sahara is the largest hot desert in the world. It covers nearly a third of Africa, about 3.6 million square miles (9.3 million sq km). During summer days, it's not unusual for the temperature in this desert to rise above 120 degrees Fahrenheit (49 degrees Celsius). Rain is very rare, and when it does rain, it's usually a big storm.

Fast Fact

The name Sahara comes from the Arabic word for desert. Arabic is a major world language that came to Africa from the Middle East more than 1,000 years ago.

The Sahara wasn't always the arid landscape it is today. About 11,000 years ago, the land was green, with many plants and bodies of water. Over time, desertification—

the process by which fertile land becomes a desert—changed this region completely.

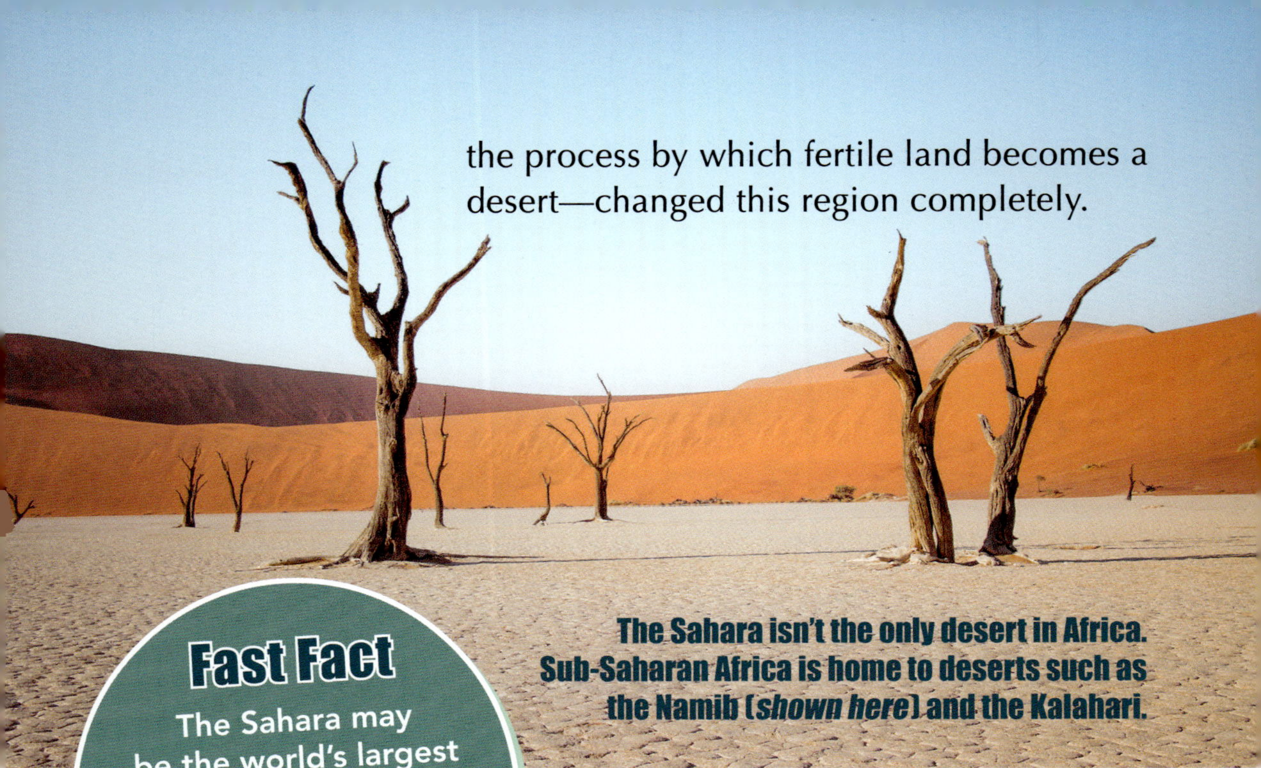

The Sahara isn't the only desert in Africa. Sub-Saharan Africa is home to deserts such as the Namib (*shown here*) and the Kalahari.

Fast Fact

The Sahara may be the world's largest hot desert, but it's not the largest desert overall—the cold deserts of the Arctic and Antarctica are larger.

Major Rivers

While there are huge areas of desert in sub-Saharan Africa, there are also mighty rivers that cut through these lands. The longest is the Nile River, which flows about 4,130 miles (6,646.6 km) from south of the equator north to the Mediterranean Sea. It cuts through 11 countries, including the sub-Saharan countries of Uganda and South Sudan.

Fast Fact

The Nile River's drainage basin was the home of a number of advanced ancient cultures, including the ancient Egyptian civilization. A drainage basin is the area where all the waterways in a region come together in a single place, such as the mouth of a river.

Shown here are lands along the Congo River. This river's basin has one of the largest rainforests in the world—second only to the Amazon Rainforest of South America.

The Congo is the second-longest river in Africa. It's about 2,900 miles (4,667.1 km) long. The Congo has many tributaries—streams or smaller rivers—that feed into it. These make up Africa's biggest network of waterways used for transportation.

Geography and Settlement

Sub-Saharan Africa's geography has played a big part in determining where people have settled across the continent. The continent's deserts make some of the land inhospitable, or difficult to live on. Some people do live in the deserts, but the population is rather small compared to other places.

Early peoples in Africa tended to settle near water sources, including the edges of lakes, in river basins, and in some coastal regions. The highland areas in eastern Africa, which get more rainfall, also drew groups of people with the promise of fertile lands for farming and more comfortable temperatures.

LAKE VICTORIA

Sub-Saharan Africa has many lakes. However, one stands out for its importance in the region. Africa's largest lake, Lake Victoria, lies on a plateau in Tanzania and Uganda, near Kenya. It's the second-largest freshwater lake in the world.

Lake Victoria is the center of one of the most densely populated spots in sub-Saharan Africa. Millions of people live near its shores. This poses a threat to the lake's ecosystem, as large populations often lead to large amounts of pollution. This can harm the fish living in the lake, as well as the people who rely on it for drinking water.

Many people carry water from Lake Victoria back to their homes to use for drinking, cooking, and washing.

Farming is an important part of life for many people in sub-Saharan Africa, and it has been since ancient times. The search for good farmland brought people closer to water sources and areas of higher rainfall.

Dangerous Desertification

In general, people do not want to live in deserts, especially ones as inhospitable as the Sahara. However, in some parts of Africa, the desert is creeping closer to where people have settled. More than 788 million acres (318.9 million ha) of land in Africa are at risk of being affected by desertification.

Desertification has happened in Africa throughout its history, but human actions have sped up the process in recent years. It can be caused by human-related climate change and by other activities, such as overgrazing animals on the land and removing trees and other plants.

The Great Green Wall is a project to plant a wall of trees at the southern edge of the Sahara to help fight desertification. Shown here are trees planted as part of this project.

Sub-Saharan Africa has many impressive geographic features, including Victoria Falls (*shown here*). This waterfall is found on the Zambezi River between Zambia and Zimbabwe. It is one of the largest waterfalls in the world.

Chapter Three

HIGHS AND LOWS

Sub-Saharan Africa is a land of incredible natural variety. Similar to its great contrasts in dry and wet areas, this region also has some great contrasts in its depths and its heights. From deep rift valleys to tall mountains, the geographic extremes of sub-Saharan Africa are exciting for nature lovers to explore.

The East African Rift System

One of the most dramatic features of Africa's geography is the East African Rift System. It is one of the largest rifts anywhere on Earth's surface. A rift is a place where Earth's crust is being pulled apart, creating deep cuts in the rock formations of an area.

The East African Rift System stretches approximately 4,000 miles (6,437.4 km) across the continent. The distance from the plateaus above to the rift's valley floor averages about 2,000 to 3,000 feet (609.6 to 914.4 m) and can be as much as 9,000 feet (2,743.2 m). This area is also home to many volcanoes.

Fast Fact

The African continent is mostly made up of a large plateau, which is an area of flat land that is raised above any surrounding lands.

Valleys are found throughout the East African Rift System. In some places, steep escarpments, or cliffs, can be seen, but in others, erosion has worn down the rift's edges.

Snow-Capped Peaks

The East African Rift System has some very low points, but sub-Saharan Africa also has many areas of extremely high elevation. Mount Kilimanjaro in Tanzania soars to 19,340 feet (5,894.8 m) at its highest point. This huge mountain is composed of three volcanoes. It has a permanent ice cap on the tallest volcano, Kibo.

Shown here is a view of Mount Kilimanjaro from Kenya. Each year, many people try to climb this mountain.

Sub-Saharan Africa has other mountains and mountain ranges, too, including the Ruwenzori range bordering the Democratic Republic of the Congo and Uganda. The Drakensberg is the main mountain range of southern Africa. It is a major part of the landscape in Lesotho and South Africa.

Fast Fact

Some scientists think that global warming could melt all the snow and ice at the top of Mount Kilimanjaro by 2050.

Africa's Islands

Moving from the mountains to sea level, Africa's coastal areas feature important landforms, including the Cape of Good Hope. This rocky mass of land juts out into the Atlantic Ocean from the coast of South Africa.

Off the coast of the continent lie many islands, each with their own ecosystems. Sub-Saharan island nations include the Comoros

The island nation of São Tomé and Príncipe (*shown here*) is one of the smallest countries in all of Africa, by both area and population.

Islands and Mauritius to the southeast in the Indian Ocean. Western islands include Cape Verde and São Tomé and Príncipe, which are in the Atlantic Ocean. Other islands not far from the African mainland include territories still claimed by European countries, such as Spain and Portugal.

Fast Fact

The Seychelles make up an island nation that is the smallest independent country in Africa by area.

The Largest Island

The biggest African island is Madagascar. It lies in the Indian Ocean off the southeastern coast of Africa, about 250 miles (402.3 km) from the shore. Although it is considered a sub-Saharan African country, the people of Madagascar are more closely related to the people of Indonesia in Southeast Asia.

Madagascar is a fairly isolated island, so many of the animals that **evolved** there didn't evolve anywhere else. It is also home to more than 11,000 species of native plants.

Lemurs, such as those shown here, are the most famous animal native to Madagascar. However, many other animals can only be found in the wild on this island as well.

DEADLY DISASTERS

Sub-Saharan Africa has a wide variety of natural features and climate zones. However, this means it is **vulnerable** to a wide variety of natural disasters and deadly weather events.

On a continent marked by large dry areas, it's probably not surprising that droughts can have a major impact on the land—and on the people, animals, and plants that live there. In sub-Saharan Africa, droughts are now happening more often. Over the years, earthquakes and flooding have done a lot of damage in parts of Africa too. Cyclones—powerful tropical storms—have hit Madagascar and other areas, killing hundreds of people.

Natural disasters in sub-Saharan Africa, especially droughts and floods, have made it hard for people to get enough food. Millions of people in this region are at risk of starvation, or dying because they don't have food to eat.

Sub-Saharan Africa is rich in natural resources, and these resources have played an important part in the history of this region. Fertile soil is one important resource, and it allows farmers to grow crops to sell in markets such as the one shown here.

Chapter Four

PAST AND PRESENT

Sub-Saharan Africa is home to a large number of natural resources, including **fossil fuels** and ores, or metals. It contains a wealth of plant life and wildlife as well, some of which can't be found anywhere else. This region also gave rise to a unique creature that would go on to spread across the world: *Homo sapiens*, or human beings. The **relationship** between these creatures and the land has affected this continent since the earliest days of humanity.

The First Humans

Human ancestors lived in sub-Saharan Africa as many as 4 million years ago, according to some scientists. Then, it is believed that *Homo sapiens* evolved around 200,000 to 300,000 years ago in this area. Some scientists think *Homo sapiens* developed in one spot in eastern sub-Saharan Africa. Others think humans evolved independently in several different places in Africa.

Fast Fact

According to most scientists, people have lived in Africa longer than they've lived anywhere else in the world.

One area of South Africa (*shown here*) is known as the Cradle of Humankind. This is because it contains the world's largest known collection of the remains of humanity's ancestors.

Geographic barriers—such as the rift system, deserts, and forests— made it hard for early humans to move around. However, migration within Africa became a part of life over time. Eventually, some early humans left the continent and began to settle in other areas around the world.

Colonizing the Continent

Sub-Saharan Africa existed as a land of strong kingdoms and advanced civilizations for centuries, but when Europeans arrived in the late 1400s CE, they changed life in the region forever. They kidnapped Africans and forcibly sent them to Europe—and later, to the Americas—where they were enslaved. More than 10 million Africans were forced from their homes in this manner.

Fast Fact

For many years, white people, the descendants of colonizers, controlled South Africa and separated its citizens by race. This policy of segregation was called apartheid, and it lasted until the 1990s.

AN IMPORTANT ADAPTATION

Living things must adapt to their environment in order to survive, and this is true for humans too. The **Indigenous** peoples of sub-Saharan Africa developed an amazing adaptation to their hot, sunny climate—their skin color. Many Africans have skin that is dark in color, although the tone of it varies widely. Darker skin has more melanin, a pigment that protects people from harmful sun rays. Groups from areas where the sun's light is most intense tend to have darker skin, while those from colder areas further from the equator often have lighter skin.

Africa has one of the most diverse populations in the world, with the most variety in its people's **DNA**. Scientists believe this is because Africa has so many different environments and climates, so people developed a variety of adaptations to live in different parts of the continent.

By the late 1800s, a race to colonize the African continent for its resources had begun. Colonizers came from many European countries, including Belgium, France, and Great Britain. The effects of this period are still felt today.

Population Problems

As the era of colonization gave way to the era of independence, urbanization took hold of sub-Saharan Africa, with many people moving to cities to find work. Urbanization combined with rapid population growth has had a big impact on the land in this region.

Clearing land to build cities has called for trees and other plants to be removed from large areas of the region. This takes away an important defense against desertification. In addition, city life is often powered by fossil fuels, which play a part in climate change. Finding ways to support a growing population while still protecting the land is essential for the future of this region.

The European colonizers didn't pay attention to existing borders and cultural groups when dividing the African continent among themselves. This led to big problems when the colonies gained independence. Conflict between different groups is a part of life in many sub-Saharan African nations because of this.

Sub-Saharan Africa's cities, such as Cape Town in South Africa (*shown here*), are often very crowded.

Hope for the Future

Sub-Saharan Africa is believed to be the home of the first humans, but it is also one of the youngest regions on Earth in terms of its population today. More than 70 percent of the people living there are under the age of 30, according to the UN. These young people have many hopes and dreams for their region's future.

Many of those dreams involve protecting the lands of sub-Saharan Africa so future generations can continue to call this region home. The people of sub-Saharan Africa have worked with their geography for thousands of years, and they hope to continue to do so far into the future.

Fast Fact

More than 26 percent of the world's refugee population lives in sub-Saharan Africa. Refugees are people who leave their home country to escape dangers such as violence and war.

Young people in sub-Saharan Africa, like the ones shown here, are speaking out about the importance of taking care of the land instead of harming it.

SUB-SAHARAN AFRICA BY THE NUMBERS

Largest Country (by Area)

Democratic Republic of the Congo: 905,000 square miles (2.3 million sq km)

Most Populated Country

Nigeria: 228 million people

Smallest Country (by Area)

Seychelles: 175 square miles (453 sq km)

Highest Point

Mount Kilimanjaro: 19,340 feet (5,894.8 m)

Longest River

Nile River: 4,130 miles (6,646.6 km)

THINK ABOUT IT!

1. What do you think about the debate surrounding the term "sub-Saharan Africa"? Do you think people speak about Africa in terms that are too general?
2. How are human actions playing a part in desertification?
3. How did the period of European colonization affect the geography of sub-Saharan Africa?
4. What are some problems sub-Saharan Africa is facing because of its growing population? Can you think of any possible solutions to those problems?

GLOSSARY

accurate: Correct.

barrier: Something that blocks, stops, or separates.

controversial: Likely to create disagreement.

culture: The beliefs and ways of life of a certain group of people.

DNA: The material in a living thing's cells that carries instructions for that living thing's basic traits.

ecosystem: A kind of natural community made up of all the living things in an area.

equator: The imaginary line that runs across the center of the earth, is an equal distance from the North Pole and South Pole, and splits the earth into the Northern Hemisphere and Southern Hemisphere.

evolve: To go through the process of evolution, or a series of changes in living things over time as they grow into new species.

fossil fuel: A fuel—such as coal, oil, or natural gas—that is formed in the earth from dead plants or animals.

Indigenous: Relating to the earliest known inhabitants of a place.

relationship: The way in which two or more people or things are connected.

United Nations: An organization formed in 1945 to promote international cooperation.

vulnerable: Open to being hurt or damaged.

FIND OUT MORE

Books

Brink, Tracy Vonder. *Africa*. New York, NY: Crabtree Publishing Company, 2023.

Jopp, Kelsey. *Africa*. Lake Elmo, MN: Focus Readers, 2021.

Klein, J. M. *The History and Government of Sub-Saharan Africa*. Buffalo, NY: PowerKids Press, 2021.

Websites

Africa: Physical Geography
education.nationalgeographic.org/resource/africa-physical-geography/
National Geographic presents a detailed overview of the geography of the entire African continent.

Satellites See Saharan Dust from Space
svs.gsfc.nasa.gov/13656/
This video from NASA shows what dust from the Sahara looks like from space.

The Scramble for Africa
www.bbc.co.uk/bitesize/articles/zrfjqfr#zqssf82
The BBC offers a closer look at the history of European colonization in Africa and its effects on the continent today.

Publisher's note to educators and parents: Our editors have carefully reviewed these websites to ensure that they are suitable for students. Many websites change frequently, however, and we cannot guarantee that a site's future contents will continue to meet our high standards of quality and educational value. Be advised that students should be closely supervised whenever they access the internet.

INDEX

The INSIDE GUIDE

GLOBAL GEOGRAPHY

TITLES IN THE SERIES

Exploring East and Southeast Asia's Geography

Exploring Europe's Geography

Exploring Latin America's Geography

Exploring Oceania's Geography

Exploring South Asia's Geography

Exploring Sub-Saharan Africa's Geography

Exploring the Geography of Russia and Its Neighbors

Exploring the Geography of the Middle East and North Africa

Exploring the Geography of the United States and Canada

ISBN: 9781502674319

9 781502 674319

Cavendish Square

Exploring the Geography of the Middle East and North Africa

The INSIDE GUIDE

GLOBAL GEOGRAPHY

Heather Smore